First published in Great Britain in 1996 by Brockhampton Press, a member of the Hodder Headline Group, 20 Bloomsbury Street, London WC1B 3QA.

This series of little gift books was made by Frances Banfield, Kate Brown, Laurel Clark, Penny Clarke, Clive Collins, Melanie Cumming, Nick Diggory, Deborah Gill, David Goodman, Douglas Hall, Maureen Hill, Nick Hutchison, John Hybert, Kate Hybert, Douglas Ingram, Simon London, Patrick McCreeth, Morse Modaberi, Tara Neill, Anne Newman, Grant Oliver, Michelle Rogers, Nigel Soper, Karen Sullivan and Nick Wells.

Compilation and selection copyright © 1996 Brockhampton Press.

All rights reserved. No part of this publication may be reproduced, stored in a retrieval system, or transmitted in any form or by any means, without the prior written permission of the copyright holder.

ISBN 1 86019 440 0

A copy of the CIP data is available from the British Library upon request.

Produced for Brockhampton Press by Flame Tree Publishing,
a part of The Foundry Creative Media Company Limited,
The Long House, Antrobus Road, Chiswick W4 5HY.

Printed and bound in Italy by L.E.G.O. Spa.

THE LITTLE BOOK OF *Love*

Selected by Beth Hurley

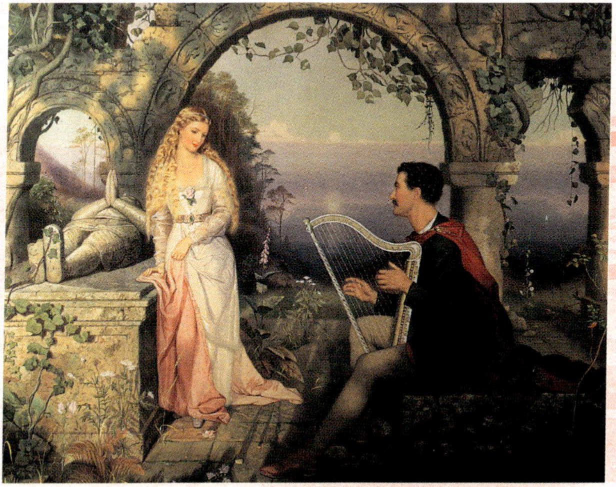

BROCKHAMPTON PRESS

How do I love thee? Let me count the ways.
I love thee to the depth and breadth and height
my soul can reach.

Elizabeth Barrett Browning

Love is a fruit in season at all times.

Mother Teresa

O the opal and the sapphire
of that wandering western sea,
And the woman riding high above
with bright hair flapping free –
The woman who I loved so,
and who loyally loved me.

Thomas Hardy, *Beeny Cliff*

Love is kisses.

Luke, 2

Love well who will, love wise who can.
Cincinnatus Heine, With Walker in Nicaragua

Ancient person, for whom I
All the flattering youth defy,
Long be it ere thou grow old,
Aching, shaking, crazy, cold;
But still continue as thou art,
Ancient person of my heart.
John Wilmot, A Song of a Young Lady to Her Ancient Lover

To love is the great amulet that makes
this world a garden.
Robert Louis Stevenson

The head never rules the heart,
but just becomes its partner in crime.
Mignon McLaughlin

The day breaks not, it is my heart.
John Donne

So far I fallen was in loves dance,
That suddenly my wit, my countenance,
My heart, my will, my nature, and my mind
Was changit right clean in another kind.
James I of Scotland, *The Kingis Quair*

To love is to admire with the heart; to admire is to love with the mind.
Théophile Gautier

The heart is a free and fetterless thing —
A wave of the ocean, a bird on the wing.
Julia Pardoe

The heart is forever inexperienced.
Henry David Thoreau

As unto the bow the cord is,
So unto the man is woman;
Though she bends him, she obeys him.
Though she draws him, yet she follows:
Useless each without the other!

Henry Wadsworth Longfellow, *The Song of Hiawatha*

The human heart, at whatever age,
opens only to the heart that opens in return.

Maria Edgeworth

You gave me the key to your heart, my love.
Then why did you make me knock?

Lord Byron

My heart shall be thy garden.

Alice Meynell

THE LITTLE BOOK OF LOVE

There is a chord in every heart
that has a sigh in it if touched aright.
Marie Louise de la Ramée

Was this the face that launch'd a thousand ships
And burnt the topless towers of Ilium?
Sweet Helen, make me immortal with a kiss.
Christopher Marlowe, *Dr Faustus*

And when love speaks, the voice of all the gods
Make heaven drowsy with the harmony.
William Shakespeare, *Love's Labour's Lost*

Love conquers all.
Virgil

I love my mummy and daddy.
I love the world.
Emma, 7

THE LITTLE BOOK OF LOVE

Dearest, in the emotion and confusion of yesterday morning, there was yet room in me for one thought which was not a feeling – for I thought that, of the many, many women who have stood where I stood, and to the same end, not one of them all perhaps, not one perhaps, since that building was a church, has had reasons strong as mine, for an absolute trust and devotion towards the man she married – not one! And then I both thought and felt, that it was only just for them ... those women who were less happy, ... to have that affectionate sympathy and support and presence of their nearest relations, parent or sister ... which failed to me, ... needing it less through being happier!

Elizabeth Barrett Browning to Robert Browning

His love was passion's essence: –
as a tree on fire by lightning with ethereal flame
kindled he was, and blasted.

Lord Byron

Is it so small a thing
To have enjoy'd the sun,
To have liv'd light in the spring,
To have lov'd, to have thought, to have done?

Matthew Arnold, *Empedocles on Etna*

Love is not getting, but giving. It is sacrifice.
And sacrifice is glorious.

Joanna Field

If a snowflake was a kiss,
I'd send you a blizzard.

Anonymous

I wish you were an old shoe
And me a piece of leather
For some old cobbler to come along
And stick us both together.

Victorian rhyme

Alas that my heart is a lute,
Whereon you have learned to play!
For many years it was mute,
Until one summer's day
You took it, and touched it, and
Made it thrill
And it thrills and throbs,
And quivers still!

Anne Lindsay

Ah, love, love! When thou seizeth us
we may well say, Goodbye prudence!

Jean de la Fontaine, *Fables*

Luve is ane fervent fire,
Kendilit without desire;
Short plesour, lang displesour,
Repentance is the hire.

Alexander Scott

At the touch of love, everyone becomes a poet.

Plato

O, speak again, bright angel! for thou art
As glorious to this night, being o'er my head,
As is a wingèd messenger of heaven
Unto the white-upturned wondering eyes
Of mortals that fall back to gaze on him
When he bestrides the lazy-pacing clouds
And sails upon the bosom of the air.

William Shakespeare, *Romeo and Juliet*

I don't love anybody but I think I might get a boyfriend at my new school.

Charlotte, 6

Where love rules, there is no will to power: and where power predominates, there love is lacking. The one is the shadow of the other.

Carl Gustav Jung, *The Psychology of the Unconscious*

Whoever loved, that loved not at first sight?
    Christopher Marlowe, *Hero and Leander*

I thank you for your gifts. All of them.
I see you are trying to teach me all the time.
I think of this when the lessons hurt. I love you.
    Alice Walker, *Living by the Word*

I'll love you, dear, I'll love you
Till China and Africa meet,
And the river jumps over the mountain ...
    W. H. Auden, *As I Walked out One Evening*

From al things in this world my hart
Has escaped but from cupits blody dart
I no resistance could find
Love is of the noblest frailty of the mind.
    Princess Mary to Francis Apsley

My heart is overflowing with just the most
unoriginal old fashiondest sort of love.

Isadora Duncan to Gordon Craig, 1904

Then you are mistaken, and you know nothing about
me, and nothing about the sort of love of which I am
capable. Every atom of your flesh is as dear to me as
my own: in pain and sickness it would still be dear.
Your mind is my treasure, and if it were broken,
it would be my treasure still: if you raved, my arms
should confine you, and not a strait waistcoat – your
grasp, even in fury, would have a charm for me:
if you flew at me as wildly as that woman did this
morning, I should receive you in an embrace,
at least as fond as it would be restrictive ...

Charlotte Brontë, *Jane Eyre*

New days, new ways,
Pass by. Love stays.

Anonymous

A JOLLY CHRISTMAS
May Christmas hours spin merrily by in mirth and goodly company.

I love you right up to the moon — AND BACK.
Sam McBratney, *Guess How Much I Love You*

All the privilege I claim for my own sex ... is that of loving longest, when existence or when hope is gone.
Jane Austen, *Persuasion*

Four be the things I'd been better without:
Love, curiosity, freckles, and doubt.
Dorothy Parker, *Enough Rope*

Love lay suddenly revealed as something equal, no
favours being asked or received, no gratitude owed.
Love was mutual hunger and shared energy,
it was laughter, hugging, relaxation,
warm satisfied sleep and waking joy.

Libby Purves, *Casting Off*

Never seek to tell thy love,
Love that never told can be;
For the gentle wind does move
Silently, invisibly.

William Blake, *Songs of Experience*

I love some people. I like the word love.

Benjamin, 6

Much ado there was, God wot;
He would love, and she would not.

Nicholas Breton, *Phillida and Coridon*

Love comes quietly ... but you know when it is there,
because suddenly ... you are not alone any more ...
and there is no sadness inside you.

Joan Walsh Anglund, *Love Is a Special Way of Feeling*

O, my Luve's like a red, red rose,
That's newly sprung in June;
O, my Luve's like the melodie
That's sweetly played in tune.

Robert Burns, *My Love Is Like a Red, Red Rose*

And Jacob served seven years for Rachel: and they
seemed unto him but a few days,
for the love he had to her.

Genesis, XXIX:20

When somebody marries somebody
they say they love each other.

Hannah, 4

LOVE: a temporary insanity curable by marriage.
  Anonymous

Love means never having to say you're sorry.
  Erich Segal, *Love Story*

But the lark is so brimful of gladness and love,
The green fields below him, the blue sky above,
That he sings, and he sings; and for ever sings he —
'I love my Love, and my Love loves me!'
  Samuel Taylor Coleridge, *Answer to a Child's Question*

My heart is like a rainbow shell
That paddles in a halcyon sea;
My heart is gladder than all these,
Because my love is come to me.
  Christina Rossetti, *A Birthday*

Love is the answer.
  John Lennon

Love is anterior to life,
Posterior to death,
Initial of creation, and
The Exponent of breath.
Emily Dickinson, *Love Is Anterior to Life*

Love turns one person into two;
and two into one.
Isaac Abravanel

I love it, I love it: and who shall dare
To chide me from loving that old armchair?
Eliza Cook, *The Old Armchair*

But love is blind, and lovers cannot see
The pretty follies that themselves commit.
William Shakespeare, *The Merchant of Venice*

Kissing don't last: cookery do!
George Meredith, *The Ordeal of Richard Feverel*

And I shall find some girl perhaps,
And a better one than you, ...
And I dare say she will do.
Rupert Brooke, *The Chilterns*

Love is enough: though the world be a-waning,
And the woods have no voice
but the voice of complaining.
William Morris, *Love Is Enough*

One turf shall serve as pillow
for us both;
One heart, one bed, two bosoms
and one troth.
William Shakespeare

Love is the wisdom of the fool
and the folly of the wise.
Samuel Johnson

To tax and to please,
no more than to love and to be wise,
is not given to men.

Edmund Burke

Love fled
And paced upon the mountains overhead
And hid his face amid a crowd of stars.

W. B. Yeats, *When You Are Old*

Love is my religion – I could die for that.

John Keats to Fanny Brawne

And sadly reflecting
That a lover forsaken
A new love may get,
But a neck when once broken
Can never be set.

William Walsh, *The Despairing Lover*

THE LITTLE BOOK OF LOVE

O tell her, brief is life but love is long.
    Alfred, Lord Tennyson, *The Princess*

I do not love thee, Dr Fell,
But why this is I cannot tell:
But this I know, I know full well,
I do not love thee, Dr Fell.
    Thomas Brown, translation of an epigram by Martial

Such a morning it is when love
leans through geranium windows
and calls with a cockerel's tongue.
    Laurie Lee, *Day of these Days*

Can you keep the bee from ranging,
Or the ringdove's neck from changing?
No! nor fetter'd Love from dying
In the knot there's no untying.
    Thomas Campbell, *Freedom and Love*

God is Love, I dare say.
But what a mischievous devil Love is.

Samuel Butler

It's never too late to have a fling,
For Autumn is just as nice as Spring,
And it's never too late to fall in love.

Sandy Wilson, 'It's Never Too Late To Fall in Love'

Marriage is the result of the longing for the deep, deep peace of the double bed after the hurly-burly of the *chaise longue*.

Mrs Patrick Campbell

Why did the acrobat get married?
Because he was head over heels in love.

Sophie, 7

Alas! the love of women! It is known
To be a lovely and fearful thing.

Lord Byron

Perfect love casteth out fear.

John, IV:20

I got a valentine from Jimmy
Jimmy
Tillie
Billie
Nicky
Mickey
Ricky
Dicky
Laura
Nora
Cora
Flora
Donnie
Ronnie
Lonnie
Connie
Eva even sent me two
But I didn't get none from you.

Shel Silverstein

The magic of first love is
our ignorance that it can ever end.

Benjamin Disraeli, *Henrietta Temple*

'Twas the voice of the sweet dove
I heard him move
heard him cry
Love, love.

Stevie Smith

I love you, I love you,
I love you divine,
Please give me your bubble gum,
You're sitting on mine.

Anonymous

Love is something you do when you get married.
Except for me, because I love my mummy.

Cole, 5

Two People

She reads the paper
While he turns on TV,
She likes the mountains,
He craves the sea
He'd rather drive,
She'll take the plane,
He waits for sunshine;
She walks in the rain.
He gulps down cold drinks,
She sips at hot;
He asks, 'Why go?'
She asks, 'Why not?'
In just about everything
They disagree
But they love one another
And they both love me.

Eve Merriam

THE LITTLE BOOK OF LOVE

Sweet Love of youth, if I forget thee
While the World's tide is bearing me along:
Sterner desires and darker hopes beset me,
Hopes which obscure but cannot do thee wrong.

Emily Brontë, *Remembrance*

I thought when love for you died,
I should die. It's dead.
Alone, most strangely, I live on.

Rupert Brooke, *The Life Beyond*

Love exists ... real love ... not the kind that depends on who you are or how you look or whether or not you are kind to someone. This meeting – this sharing – this naked confrontation where two beings are, for an instant, together.

Leslie Kenton

I love thee, though I told thee not,
Right easily and long,
Thou wert my joy in every spot,
My theme in every song.

John Clare

We poor, common folk must take wives whom we love and who love us.

Wolfgang Amadeus Mozart

Amo, Amas, I love a lass
As a cedar tall and slender;
Sweet cowslip's grave is her nominative case,
And she's of the feminine gender.

John O'Keefe

I wish I was either in your arms full of faith or that a thunderbolt would strike me.

John Keats

There is no greater wonder than the way the face of a young woman fits in a man's mind, and stays there, and he could never tell you why; it just seems it was the thing he wanted.

Robert Louis Stevenson

But a woman's words to a lusting lover
Should be written in wind and running water.

Catullus

Say, what is the spell,
when her fledgelings are cheeping,
That lures the bird home to her nest?
Or wakes the tired mother,
whose infant is weeping,
To cuddle and croon it to rest?
What's the magic that charms
the glad babe in her arms,
Till it coos with the voice of the dove?
'Tis a secret,
and so let us whisper it low –
And the name of the secret is LOVE!
For I think it is Love,
For I feel it is Love,
For I'm sure it is nothing
but LOVE!

Lewis Carroll

THE LITTLE BOOK OF LOVE

Though I speak with the tongues of men and angels, and have not charity, I am become as sounding brass, or a tinkling cymbal. And though I have the gift of prophecy, and understand all mysteries, and knowledge; and though I have all faith, so that I could remove mountains, and have not charity, I am nothing.

I Corinthians, XIII:1–2

Come live with me, and be my love,
And we will all the pleasures prove,
That valleys, groves, hills and fields,
Woods or steepy mountain yields.

Christopher Marlowe, *The Passionate Shepherd to His Love*

It is easier to be a lover than a husband for the simple reason that it is more difficult to be witty every day than to say pretty things from time to time.

Honoré de Balzac

Notes on Illustrations

Page 5 *The Serenade*, by John Simmons (City of Bristol Museum & Art Gallery). Courtesy of The Bridgeman Art Library; **Page 6** *June Roses*, by Gunning King (John Noott Galleries, Broadway, Worcestershire). Courtesy of The Bridgeman Art Library; **Page 8-9** *The Sea*, by Povl Steffenson (Christie's, London). Courtesy of The Bridgeman Art Library; **Page 11** 'Love's Garland to Thee', Victorian Valentine Card (Hereford City Museum and Art Gallery). Courtesy of The Bridgeman Art Library; **Page 12** *The Magpie Picture Gallery*. Courtesy of The Laurel Clark Collection; **Page 15** *Signing the Marriage Registrar*, by James Charles (Bradford Art Galleries & Museums). Courtesy of The Bridgeman Art Library; **Page 17** *The Sonnet*, by William Mulready (Victoria & Albert Museum, London). Courtesy of The Bridgeman Art Library; **Page 19** *The Wedding Dress*, by Frederick Daniel Hardy (Oldham Art Gallery, Lancashire). Courtesy of The Bridgeman Art Library; **Page 20** *The Love of Paris & Helen*, by Jacques Louis David (Louvre, Paris). Courtesy of The Bridgeman Art Library; **Page 22** *Mother's Kiss*. Courtesy of The Laurel Clark Collection; **Page 25** *The Kiss*, by G. Baldry (Simon Carter Gallery, Woodbridge). Courtesy of The Bridgeman Art Library; **Page 27** *The Orchard*, by Nelly Erichsen (Roy Miles Gallery, London). Courtesy of The Bridgeman Art Library; **Page 28** *A Jolly Christmas, Mr & Mrs Snowman*. Courtesy of The Laurel Clark Collection; **Page 32-3** *A Romantic Evening*, by Charles Spenelayh (Roy Miles Fine Paintings, London). Courtesy of The Bridgeman Art Library; **Page 36** *I Will*, by François Brunery (Towneley Hall Art Gallery & Museum, Burnley). Courtesy of The Bridgeman Art Library; **Page 38-9** *The Wedding Party*, by Matteo Meneghini (Dreweatt Neate Fine Art Auctioneers, Newbury). Courtesy of The Bridgeman Art Library; **Page 41** 'To My Valentine', Victorian Valentine Card (Private Collection). Courtesy of The Bridgeman Art Library; **Page 42** *Ruba'iyat of Omar Khayyam: A Love*, by Rene Bull (British Library, London). Courtesy of The Bridgeman Art Library; **Page 44** *The Pride of Dijon*, by W. J. Hennesy (Cooley Gallery, Old Lyme, Connecticut). Courtesy of The Bridgeman Art Library; **Page 46** *All Things Love Thee: So Do I*. Courtesy of The Laurel Clark Collection; **Page 48** *The Fisherman's Wooing*, by Eugene de Blaas (A. & F. Pears Ltd, London). Courtesy of The Bridgeman Art Library; **Page 51** 'And She Very Imprudently Married the Barber' from *The Panjandrum Picture Book*, published by Frederick Warne & Co. (Central Saint Martins College of Art). Courtesy of The Bridgeman Art Library; **Page 52-3** *Jealousy and Flirtation*, by Haynes King (Victoria & Albert Museum, London). Courtesy of The Bridgeman Art Library; **Page 55** *Ode To the First of May*, from *The French of Jean Passerat*. Courtesy of The Laurel Clark Collection; **Page 56** *Lovers Embracing on a Terrace* (Private Collection). Courtesy of The Bridgeman Art Library; **Page 58** *The Serenade*, by John Simmons (City of Bristol Museum & Art Gallery). Courtesy of The Bridgeman Art Library.

Acknowledgements: The Publishers wish to thank everyone who gave permission to reproduce the quotes in this book. Every effort has been made to contact the copyright holders, but in the event that an oversight has occurred, the publishers would be delighted to rectify any omissions in future editions of this book. Children's quotes printed courtesy of Herne Hill School; *Living by the Word*, Alice Walker, reprinted courtesy of Vintage; W.H. Auden, reprinted courtesy of Faber & Faber; *Casting Off*, Libby Purves, reprinted courtesy of HodderHeadline; *The Chilterns*, Rupert Brooke, from *The Collected Poems of Rupert Brooke*, reprinted courtesy of Sidgwick & Jackson, a part of Pan Macmillan; *When You Are Old*, W.B. Yeats, reprinted courtesy of A.P. Watt; *Day of these Days*, Laurie Lee, reprinted courtesy of Andre Deutsch and Peters, Fraser and Dunlop Group; Stevie Smith reprinted courtesy of Penguin Books; *The Life Beyond*, Rupert Brooke, from *The Collected Poems of Rupert Brooke*, reprinted courtesy of Sidgwick & Jackson, a part of Pan Macmillan.